Nelson

ENGLISH

DEVELOPMENT

BOOK 2

JOHN JACKMAN
WENDY WREN

Nelson

Contents

Writing		Working with words
planning a story – plot	beginning/middle/end	adjectives with several meanings
imaginative personal	lists descriptive	classification – fruit/vegetables animal babies
lists matching pictures and text instructions	personal preference imaginative	matching – food words
planning a story – when? sentence completion	descriptive imaginative	looking at languages – Old Norse
classification factual personal preference	descriptive imaginative	dictionary work – wheel words
personal recording information – graph plot/story structure	finishing a story imaginative	classifying – verbs dictionary work
imaginative drawing/labelling maps	personal letters descriptive	extending vocabulary – nouns and verbs dictionary work
imaginative descriptive	diary extract	classification – nouns dictionary work
finishing a story imaginative planning a story – characters	recording information – chart sentence writing research/factual	matching – people and countries
planning a story – setting descriptive	book covers sentence writing	classifying – adjectives extending vocabulary
book covers		looking at languages – Latin and Greek dictionary work
diary entries based on pictures personal/record keeping	imaginative	extending vocabulary – occupations
imaginative diary extract	research	extending vocabulary – adverbs
research note taking	imaginative personal	words from 'encyclopedia' nouns and adjectives
finishing a story imaginative	descriptive	extending vocabulary – opposites with prefix 'in'

Greeks and Trojans

The ancient Greeks fought many wars and had many heroes. One of the most famous wars was against the Trojans. Troy, where the Trojans lived, was a walled city ruled by King Priam. The Greeks built a camp outside the city. For ten years they tried to capture Troy. This is how the Greeks won the Trojan war.

The Wooden Horse

Morning dawned over the windy plain of Troy, and the Trojans looked out towards the great camp of the Greeks which had stood there so long – looked, and rubbed their eyes and looked again.

'The Greeks have indeed gone!' they cried. 'The camp lies in ashes; there is not a man, not a ship to be seen. But there stands in the midst of the ruins a great Wooden Horse the like of which we have never seen.'

Then the gates of Troy were flung open and out poured young and old, laughing and shouting in their joy that the Greeks were gone at last. They came to the ruined camp and stood gazing at the great Wooden Horse.

At once a great argument broke out among the Trojans as to what should be done with the Horse. Some wanted to take it inside the city. Some wanted to fling it into the sea. It was decided to take the Wooden Horse into Troy. They dragged it across the plain but when they reached the gate of the city, the Horse proved too big to enter by it. The Trojans pulled down a section of the wall and brought it into the middle of Troy.

Night fell, and the Trojans feasted in their joy that the Great War was over and the Greeks had gone. At last worn out with excitement and celebration, they fell asleep, leaving few guards by the walls and gates.

Inside the Horse the Greeks were sitting trembling and alert. When the first light of morning came they undid the bolt and opened the door in the Horse. They climbed down, crept through the silent streets, killed the sleepy guards and opened the gates to the armies of the Greeks who had sailed back to Troy in the dead of night!

Adapted from *The Tale of Troy* by Roger Lancelyn Green

Glossary
a *glossary* explains what a word means
midst means middle

COMPREHENSION

Read the passage and answer the questions.

1 Who was the King of Troy?

2 How do you think the Trojans felt when they saw that the Greeks had gone?

3 What did the Trojans do with the Wooden Horse?

4 Who was inside the Wooden Horse?

5 What did they do?

6 How do you think the Trojans felt when they woke up to find the Greeks inside the city?

PLANNING A STORY – WHAT HAPPENS?

Before you begin to write a story you need to plan **what** is going to happen.

You need to plan how your story begins.
You need to plan what happens in the middle of your story.
You need to plan how you are going to end your story.

This is called the **plot**.

Look at the **plot** of 'The Wooden Horse'.

Beginning

The Trojans wake up to find the Greek camp empty and a huge Wooden Horse left outside their city.

Middle

The Trojans talk about what they should do with the Horse. They bring it into the city and celebrate. When they go to sleep they do not guard the walls and gates very well.

End

The Greeks are inside the Horse.
Just before morning they come out of the Horse and capture the city of Troy.

The pictures below tell a story called 'The Big Bully'.

Beginning of the story   Middle of the story

End of the story

1 Write the **plot** of this story by saying what is happening in each picture.

2 Think about a story you could write called 'The Hide-out'. Write the **plot** of the story.

- How does your story begin?
- What happens in the middle of your story?
- How does your story end?

WORKING WITH WORDS

In the story the Greeks left a 'great Wooden Horse' outside the city of Troy.

Great is an adjective ('describing' word) with three meanings:

large   very good   important

1 Which meaning is the best for 'great Wooden Horse'?

2 Write three sentences of your own using the word **great** to show each meaning.

7

Food on a farm

Lots of farmers grow fruit and vegetables that people can now pick themselves. You can often go and pick your own strawberries.

I liked growing

I liked growing.
That was nice.
The leaves were soft
The sun was hot.
I was warm and red and round
Then someone dropped me in a pot.

Being a strawberry isn't all pleasing.
This morning they put me in ice cream.
I'm freezing.

Karla Kuskin

COMPREHENSION   Read the poem and answer the questions.

1 Why did the strawberry like growing?

2 Describe what the strawberry looked like when it was growing.

3 What happened to the strawberry?

4 Why wasn't the strawberry very pleased?

5 How else could you eat strawberries besides with ice cream?

If you could be a fruit or a vegetable what would you be?

1 Write about what you look like.
   ● Think about your colour, shape and size.
   ● Are you smooth or knobbly?
   ● Are you a bright colour, a dull colour or lots
     of colours?

2 Write about where you grow.
   ● Do you grow underground or above the ground?
   ● Do you grow on a tree?

3 Write about what happens to you after you are picked
   and before you are eaten.
   ● Are you peeled?
   ● Are you chopped or are you mashed?
   ● Are you cooked? How are you cooked?

ANIMAL VERBS

If I were a pig

If I were a pig and lived under a thatch
With nothing to do but gobble and scratch,
How nice it would be to look out now and then
And see the great winds blowing over the fen.

Elizabeth Fleming

Glossary
fen means low, wet land – a marsh

The words **gobble** and **scratch** are verbs ('doing' words).
They tell us what the pig does.
Make a list of as many farm animals as you can.
Now think of verbs to say what they do, how they eat and the
noises they make, like this:

animal	verb
pig	gobbles, scratches

Meadow Avenue

The yields
of fields
were cows and crops

But now
No cows:
Just streets and shops.

Trevor Millum

Glossary

yield means what the fields give us

COMPREHENSION

Read the poem and answer the questions.

1 What has happened to the cows and the crops?

2 Do you think the poet is pleased about what has happened?

3 Why do we need cows and crops?

4 Why do we need streets and shops?

5 If we need them both, what should we do about it?

1   Look at the picture of the market stall.
    It sells fruit, vegetables and salad crops.

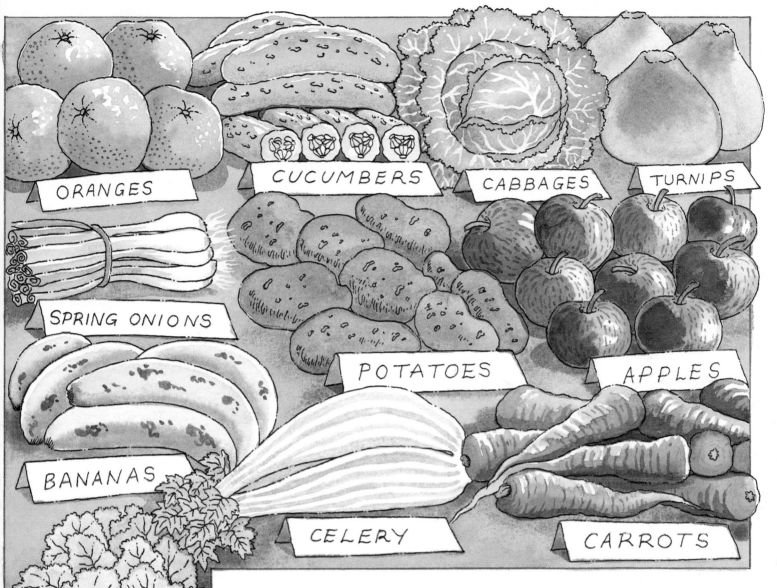

Copy these headings into your book.

fruit   vegetables   salad crops

Put the words from the picture under the right heading.
Can you add some more words to the lists?

2   Baby animals have special names.
    What do we call these baby animals?

a young cow   a young sheep
a young duck   a young horse
a young hen   a young goat
a young pig   a young goose

Food, glorious food!

The Mad Hatter's tea party

Alice meets the Mad Hatter and the March Hare at a very odd tea party.

There was a table set out under a tree in front of the house, and the March Hare and the Hatter were having tea at it; a Dormouse was sitting between them, fast asleep, and the other two were using it as a cushion, resting their elbows on it, and talking over its head. "Very uncomfortable for the Dormouse," thought Alice; "only, as it's asleep, I suppose it doesn't mind."

The table was a large one, but the three were all crowded together at one corner of it. "No room! No room!" they cried out when they saw Alice coming.

"There's *plenty* of room!" said Alice indignantly, and she sat down in a large arm-chair at one end of the table.

"Have some wine," the March Hare said in an encouraging tone.

Alice looked all round the table, but there was nothing on it but tea. "I don't see any wine," she remarked.

"There isn't any," said the March Hare.

From *Alice in Wonderland* by Lewis Carroll

Glossary
indignantly means angrily

COMPREHENSION

Read the passage and answer the questions.

1 Where were the Mad Hatter and the March Hare having tea?

2 Where was the Dormouse?

3 What did the March Hare offer to Alice?

4 Why was this an odd thing to do?

5 What do you think Alice thought about the March Hare and his friends?

LET'S HAVE A PARTY!

The Mad Hatter's tea party wasn't much of a party.
There was only tea to drink and no food!
Write a list of food and drink you think the Mad Hatter should have had at his party.

FOLLOWING INSTRUCTIONS

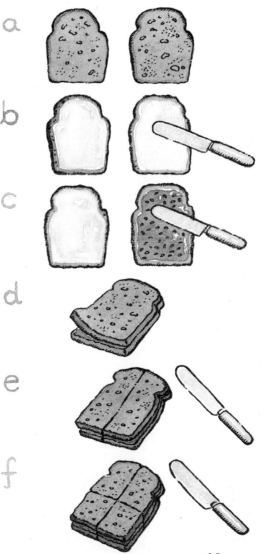

1 Look at the pictures.
They show you how to make a jam sandwich.

The sentences that go with the pictures are muddled up.
Match the sentences with the pictures.
The first one is done for you.

a Get two slices of bread.

Put the two slices of bread together.
Put butter or margarine on each slice.
Cut the bread in half.
Get two slices of bread.
Cut each half in half again.
Put jam on one slice.

2 Write step-by-step instructions for one of these:

getting a bowl of cereal ready for breakfast
getting a special meal for a pet

READING A MENU

People sometimes go out to a restaurant to eat.
They choose what they want to eat by looking at a menu.
Look:

Look at what you can have for your main meal.

1 If you want an Italian meal, what will you choose?

2 If you want an Indian meal, what will you choose?

3 If you want a meal without meat, what will you choose?

Look at what you can have for dessert.

4 If you want something with fruit in, what will you choose?

5 If you want cake, what will you choose?

6 If you want a cold dessert, what will you choose?

WRITING A MENU

Imagine you have your own restaurant.
Choose a name for your restaurant.
Write a menu with three things to choose from for the main meal and three things to choose from for the dessert.
Set out your menu like the one for The Dormouse Diner.

A REALLY HORRIBLE MEAL

Here is part of a poem by Roald Dahl called 'The Centipede's Song'.
The centipede is telling us about the sorts of things he eats.

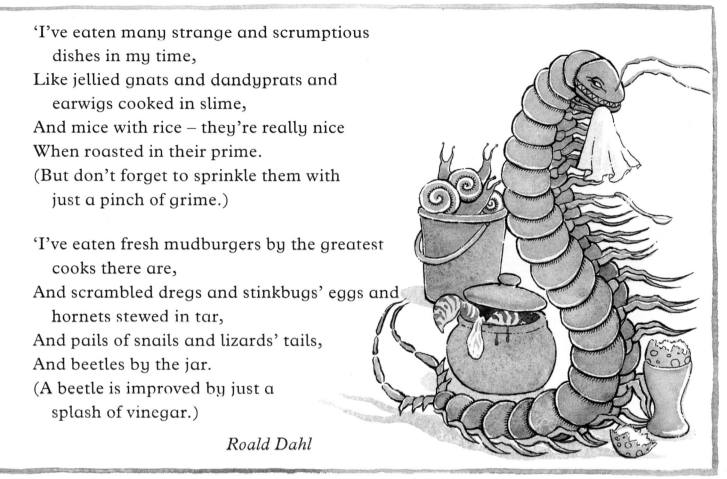

'I've eaten many strange and scrumptious
    dishes in my time,
Like jellied gnats and dandyprats and
    earwigs cooked in slime,
And mice with rice – they're really nice
When roasted in their prime.
(But don't forget to sprinkle them with
    just a pinch of grime.)

'I've eaten fresh mudburgers by the greatest
    cooks there are,
And scrambled dregs and stinkbugs' eggs and
    hornets stewed in tar,
And pails of snails and lizards' tails,
And beetles by the jar.
(A beetle is improved by just a
    splash of vinegar.)

Roald Dahl

Imagine you are a large, hungry minibeast.
Make up a list of horrible things that you would like to eat!

WORKING WITH WORDS

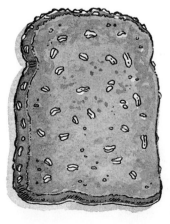

Some foods go together.
Copy the lists.
Can you put the right foods together?
One is done to help you.

toast	rice
bread	cream
salt	egg
peaches	chips
bacon	marmalade
fish	butter
curry	pepper

The Vikings

The Vikings were very good at shipbuilding and sailing. They sailed to many lands including Russia, Britain and even America. This is the beginning of a story called *The Saga of Erik the Viking*. Erik wanted to sail to a very unusual place.

The Saga of Erik the Viking

This is a tale of a Viking warrior who lived hundreds and hundreds of years ago. His name was Erik. His ship was called Golden Dragon, and its figurehead was a fierce monster carved out of wood, and covered with gold leaf.

One day Erik said to his wife: 'I must find the land where the sun goes at night.' But his wife replied: 'No one has ever been to that far country. And of those who have tried few have ever returned.'

'You are right,' said Erik, 'but, until I have sought that distant land, I shall never sleep in my bed again.'

So he called his son who was fifteen years old and told him he must guard their home by day and night. Then he took his sword, which was called Blueblade, stepped on board Golden Dragon and sailed off towards the setting sun . . .

The next morning they found themselves alone on the ocean with great waves heaving the ship up and down. Erik looked up into the sky and smelt the wind.

'We shan't make it!' whispered Erik's men, one to the other, as the storm clouds blotted out the sun.

Terry Jones

Glossary
a *saga* is the story of a hero
sought means looked for

Read the passage and answer the questions.

1 What do you think a warrior was?

2 Where on a ship would you find the figurehead?

3 How do you think that Erik's wife felt about Erik going on this journey?

4 Do you think that Erik would ever find 'the land where the sun goes at night'?

STORY BEGINNINGS

The beginning of a story sometimes tells us **when** the story happened.

The first sentence of *The Saga of Erik the Viking* tells us that the story happened a long time ago.

'This is a tale of a Viking warrior who lived **hundreds and hundreds of years ago**.'

1 There are lots of words and phrases that tell us when something happened.

Look at the pictures below.

Copy and finish the sentences by describing what is happening in the pictures.

a Early in the morning . . .

b At night . . .

c One beautiful summer day . . .

d In the middle of Winter . . .

2 Here are the beginnings of some other stories.
  Write the words that tell you when the stories happened.

  a Long ago there lived a man who had lots of cats.
  b A few weeks ago there was a terrible storm.
  c One day a stranger came to the village.

PLANNING A STORY – WHEN DOES IT HAPPEN?

Before you write a story you need to plan **what** is going to happen.
You also need to plan **when** things happen in the story.

Think about a story you could write called 'The Accident'.
Use these questions to help you plan when your story happened.

- Did the story happen a long time ago?
- Is it a modern story?
- Does everything happen in a day, a week, a month, or longer?
- Does the story happen in Winter, Spring, Summer or Autumn?

A STORM AT SEA   Imagine you are one of Erik's sailors.
You are in the middle of the sea, far away
from land, and a storm is coming.

Write about what happens.

- Remember to describe:
  the storm
  what you and the other sailors did
  what happened to the ship

- Remember to write about **when** things happened.
  Think about when the storm started, how long it lasted
  and when it finished.

WORKING WITH
WORDS

The Viking language is called **Old Norse**.
Lots of the names of our towns and villages are
Old Norse names.

By is the Old Norse for farm or settlement.
Place names ending in **by** were probably where the
Vikings settled:

Der**by** and Grims**by**

1 Look at a map of Britain.
  Can you find some more places ending in **by**?
  Make a list.

2 Places ending with these words are also where Vikings
  probably settled:

  scale meaning hut or shelter
  toft meaning plot of land

  Can you find any on the map?
  Make a list.

By land, sea and air

What is transport?

The word **transport** means something that can carry people and things from one place to another. We have transport to move on the land, over the sea and through the air.

The first cars that were made went very slowly. Someone had to walk in front of them waving a flag to warn people they were coming! Now cars and other sorts of transport we see on the roads go very quickly indeed.

The train was invented in Britain in 1804. Soon it became a popular type of transport. The first trains were powered by steam. Nowadays trains run on electricity or diesel and are faster and quieter.

Boats have been built for thousands of years. Some of the earliest boats were tree trunks with the middles hollowed out. Some were made of animal skins. Today there are enormous tankers and cruiseships that sail all over the world.

The first aeroplane was built by the Wright brothers and it made its first flight on December 17th 1903. Today Concorde can fly faster than the speed of sound!

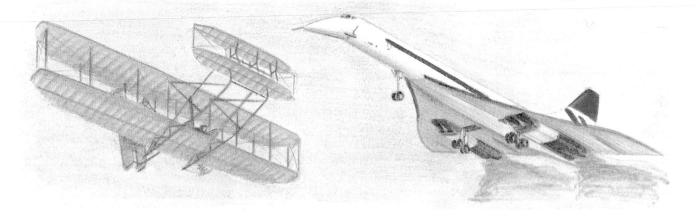

COMPREHENSION   Read the passage and answer the questions.

1   What does the word **transport** mean?

2   Cars travel on roads. What other sorts of transport use the road?

3   What is a cruiseship?

4   What is a tanker? Why do you think they are called tankers?

5   Look at the picture of the Wright brothers' plane and Concorde. What differences can you see?

6   How do you think it would feel to fly on Concorde?

CLASSIFYING

Look at the words in the box.

car	hydrofoil	jumbo jet	bus	lorry
canoe	motorbike	train	catamaran	
glider	bicycle	submarine	airliner	
cruiseship	helicopter	hot air balloon	ferry	

Copy these headings into your book.

land   **sea**   **air**

Put the words under the right heading.
Use a dictionary for the words you have not seen before.

DESCRIBING VEHICLES

Some sorts of vehicles are needed to help people do their jobs.
Look at the photographs.
These are vehicles that go on land.

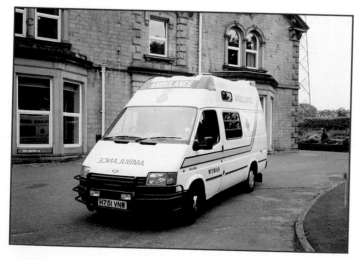

22

1 What jobs do the vehicles help people to do?
Write a sentence about the work each one is
used for.

2 Which vehicle would you like to drive?
Write about why you would like to drive it.
Write about what your vehicle looks like.
You can invent your own vehicle if you wish.

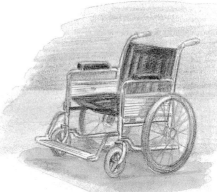

**WORKING WITH
WORDS**

Look at this list of words.
They all have **wheel** in them.
What do they mean?
Use a dictionary to help you to
describe each one in a sentence.

wheelbarrow
wheelchair
waterwheel
spinning wheel
Catherine wheel

Journeys

From a railway carriage

Faster than fairies, faster than witches,
Bridges and houses, hedges and ditches;
And charging along like troops in a battle,
All through the meadows the horses and cattle;
All of the sights of the hill and the plain
Fly as thick as driving rain;
And ever again, in the wink of an eye,
Painted stations whistle by.

Here is a child who clambers and scrambles,
All by himself and gathering brambles;
Here is a tramp who stands and gazes;
And there is the green for stringing the daisies!
Here is a cart run away in the road
Lumping along with man and load;
And here is a mill, and there is a river:
Each a glimpse and gone for ever!

Robert Louis Stevenson

COMPREHENSION   The person travelling by train is looking out of a window.
He sees lots of things as the train whizzes by.

1   Pick out the verbs in the poem that tell you what the people
    are doing.

2   What animals does he see out of the window?

3   What other things does he see out of the window?

4   What does the poet mean when he says 'in the wink of
    an eye'?

5   Look at the end of each line of the poem.
    Write the pairs of words that rhyme.

A TRAIN JOURNEY

Have you ever travelled by train?

● Where did you go?
● Did you like travelling by train?
● What did you see out of the window?

Write about your train journey.
You can invent a journey if you wish.

A TRAVEL GRAPH

Sally had to find out how the children in her class travelled to school.
She found that some of them came by car, some of them came by bicycle and some of them walked.
She made a graph to show what she had found out.

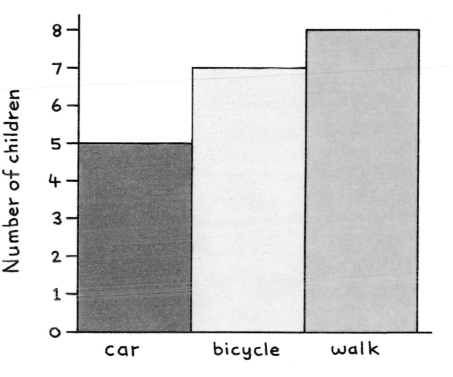

Look at the graph and answer the questions.

1 How many children travel to school by car?

2 How many children travel to school by bicycle?

3 How many children walk to school?

Now find out how the children in your class travel to school.
Make a graph to show what you have found out.

A PICTURE STORY The Lavine family are going on holiday to Spain.
They have to use five types of transport to get from their
house in New Street to the hotel in Spain.
Look at the pictures.

1

2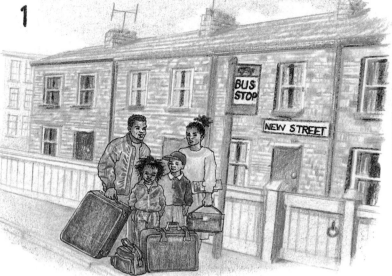

3

4

5

6

7  **8**

1 Write a sentence for each picture saying what the Lavines are doing.

When you have finished you will have written what has happened in the story. This is the **plot** of a story about the Lavines going on holiday to Spain.

2 Finish the story by deciding what happens in picture 8.

WORKING WITH WORDS

1 Different types of transport move at different speeds. People and animals move at different speeds as well. Look at the words below. Some are slow-moving words and some are fast-moving words.

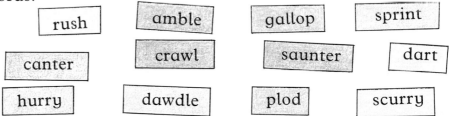

rush   amble   gallop   sprint

canter   crawl   saunter   dart

hurry   dawdle   plod   scurry

Write **fast words** and **slow words** as headings in your book.
Put the words under the right heading.
Use a dictionary for the words you have not seen before.
Can you add some words of your own?

2 Use two of the fast words and two of the slow words in sentences of your own.

Sailing westwards

Great explorers

During the 15th and 16th centuries there were many explorations. One of the reasons why men sailed across the seas was to trade. The Portuguese sailed to the southern tip of Africa and then on to India. They brought back silver, spices and other rich goods. They built forts along the east coast of Africa to stop ships from other countries reaching the rich lands of the East. People thought that the Earth was flat. They had found land by sailing east but they were afraid to cross the ocean and sail west in case they fell off the edge of the Earth.

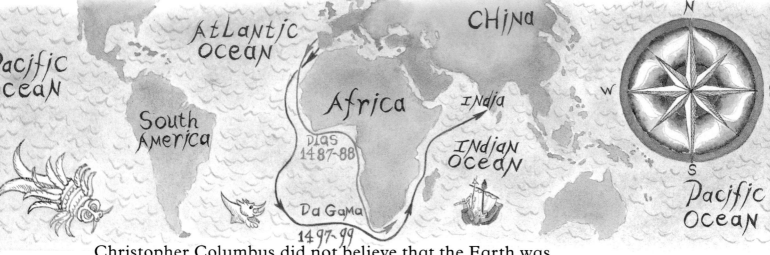

Christopher Columbus did not believe that the Earth was flat. He thought it was round and that if he sailed west he would reach India on the other side.

He was right about the Earth being round but he was wrong in thinking that the first land he would reach would be India!

After five weeks without the sight of land he reached a group of islands we now call the West Indies. The first people he encountered were the peace-loving Arawaks who thought the Spanish ships were giant birds. Columbus had landed in America. Twenty-six years later, Ferdinand Magellan found the way round the southern tip of America to the East that Columbus had been searching for.

Glossary

trade means buying and selling

COMPREHENSION

Look at the two maps and answer the questions.

1 Who reached the southern tip of Africa?

2 Who reached India?

3 Which ocean did Columbus cross?

4 Which oceans did Magellan's ships cross?

MAKING A MAP

You were able to answer the questions by looking at the maps. Maps give us a lot of information.

1 Imagine you are the captain of a ship.
You have found an island and buried your treasure to keep it safe. Draw a map of the island.
You will need to put lots of information on it.

Coastline
- Where is it safe to land your ship?
- Where are the rocky places?

Inland
- Where is there fresh water for you to drink?
- Are there mountains, forests, deep rivers?
- Are there people living on the island?
- Are they friendly or not?
- Are there wild animals?
- Where is the treasure?

2 Give your island a name.

The Aztecs

The Aztecs ruled in central and southern Mexico from 1325 to 1521.

When the Spaniard Hernán Cortés and his men arrived in Mexico in 1519 they were met by the Aztecs who rowed out to the Spanish ships. The Spaniards asked them who they were and who their king was. They answered, "Lords, we come from Mexico and our king is Montezuma." Cortés was soon to hear a lot about the fierce and powerful Aztec king. The Spanish and the Aztecs then gave each other gifts. The Aztecs gave beautiful embroidered cloth and the Spanish gave glass beads.

The Aztecs left and travelled quickly to tell their king about the strangers. They showed him the presents that Cortés had given them and also drawings they had done of the Spanish ships, guns, horses and armour.

The first meeting of the Aztecs and the Spanish was friendly but within two years, Cortés and his men had attacked and destroyed the capital city and put an end to the Aztec empire.

COMPREHENSION

Read the passage and answer the questions.

1 What part of Mexico was ruled by the Aztecs?

2 When did Cortés and his men land in Mexico?

3 What gift did the Aztecs give to Cortés?

4 What did Cortés give to the Aztecs?

5 How did the Aztecs prove to their king that the Spanish had landed?

6 Who was king of the Aztecs?

7 When was the Aztec empire destroyed?

8 What do you think the Aztecs thought when they first saw the Spanish ships?

WRITING A LETTER

Imagine you are Cortés the Spanish sailor.
You have just met the Aztecs for the first time.
Write a letter home telling your family about the Aztecs.
Remember you have just landed in a strange country.

● How were the Aztecs dressed? (The picture will help you.)
● What did they say and do? (Remember about the gifts.)
● What did you think about them?
● Are you surprised that the Aztecs are friendly?
● Did you think they would attack you?
● What do you think about their gift?
● Are you looking forward to meeting the Aztec king?

WORKING WITH WORDS

Remember **n** = noun and **v** = verb in the dictionary.

When we **explore** we make an **exploration**.

explore is a verb   **exploration** is a noun

Look up the meanings of these words in your dictionary.
Write the nouns by adding **ation**.
Use your dictionary to help you.

investigate   explain   examine

Strange creatures

Stig of the Dump

Barney goes exploring near a chalk pit he calls 'the dump', and has a very strange encounter.

Barney crawled through the rough grass and peered over. Far below was the bottom of the pit. The dump. Barney could see strange bits of wreckage among the moss and elder bushes and nettles. Was that the steering wheel of a ship? The tail of an aeroplane? At least there was a real bicycle. Barney felt sure he could make it go if only he could get at it. They didn't let him have a bicycle.

Barney wished he was at the bottom of the pit.

And the ground gave way.

Barney felt his head going down and his feet going up. There was a rattle of falling earth beneath him.

Then he was falling, still clutching the clump of grass that was falling with him.

He was lying in a kind of shelter. Looking up he could see a roof, or part of a roof, made of elder branches, a very rotten old carpet, and rusty old sheets of iron. There was a big hole, through which he must have fallen. He could see the white walls of the cliff, the trees and creepers at the top, and the sky with clouds passing over it.

It was dark in this den after looking at the white chalk, and he couldn't see what sort of place it was. It seemed to be partly a cave dug into the chalk, partly a shelter built out over the mouth of the cave.

He lay quiet and looked around the cave again. Now that his eyes were used to it he could see further into the dark part of the cave.

There was somebody there!

Or Something!

★

Something, or Somebody, had a lot of shaggy black hair and two bright black eyes that were looking very hard at Barney.

'Hullo!' said Barney.

Something said nothing.

'I fell down the cliff,' said Barney.

Somebody grunted.

'My name's Barney.'

Somebody-Something made a noise that sounded like 'Stig'.

Adapted from *Stig of the Dump* by Clive King

COMPREHENSION   Read the passage and answer the questions.

1 What could Barney see at the bottom of the pit?

2 Why did Barney want to reach the bicycle?

3 What was the shelter like that Barney had fallen into?

4 What did Stig look like?

5 How do you think Barney felt when he saw Stig?

6 Why do you think Barney called Stig 'Somebody-Something'?

7 Who or what do you think Stig is?

Five Children and It

Robert, Anthea, Jane, Cyril and Baby decide to dig a hole to see if they can reach Australia. Four of the children soon get bored but Anthea goes on digging.

Anthea suddenly screamed:

'Cyril! Come here! Oh, come quick! It's alive! It'll get away! Quick!'

They all hurried back.

'It's a rat, I shouldn't wonder,' said Robert.

'Perhaps it is a snake,' said Jane, shuddering.

'Let's look,' said Cyril, jumping into the hole. 'I'm not afraid of snakes.'

'Oh, don't be silly!' said Anthea; 'it's not a rat, it's *much* bigger. And it's not a snake. It's got feet; I saw them; and fur! It sounds silly, but it said something.'

'What?'

'It said, "You let me alone".'

Robert and Cyril dug with spades while Anthea sat on the edge of the hole, jumping up and down.

Then Anthea cried out, '*I'm* not afraid. Let me dig,' and fell on her knees and began to scratch like a dog does when he has suddenly remembered where it was that he buried his bone.

'Oh, I felt fur,' she cried. 'I did indeed! I did!' when suddenly a dry husky voice in the sand made them all jump back, and their hearts jumped nearly as fast as they did.

The children stood round the hole in a ring, looking at the creature they had found. It was worth looking at. Its eyes were on long horns like a snail's eyes. It had ears like a bat's ears, and its tubby body was shaped like a spider's and covered with thick soft fur. Its legs and arms were furry too, and it had hands and feet like a monkey's.

Adapted from *Five Children and It* by E. Nesbit

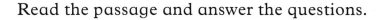

COMPREHENSION

Read the passage and answer the questions.

1 What did Robert think Anthea had found?

2 How did Anthea know that it wasn't a rat or a snake?

3 What part of the creature was like a snail?

4 What part of the creature was like a spider?

5 What part of the creature was like a bat?

6 What part of the creature was like a monkey?

7 How do you know that the children were a little bit afraid of what they had found?

STRANGE CREATURES

In *Stig of the Dump* and *Five Children and It*, the characters go exploring and encounter very strange creatures.

1 Imagine you are exploring in a wood and encounter a strange creature.
The creature is friendly and can talk to you.
When you get home you write about what has happened.

Remember to write about:
● when it happened
● where you found the creature
● what it looked like
● what you talked about

2 Draw your strange creature.

WORKING WITH WORDS

Barney goes exploring in a **chalk** pit and falls into a shelter where there are rusty old sheets of **iron**.

Chalk is a kind of rock. Iron is a kind of metal.
Look at the words below. Some are rock and some are metal.

granite   gold   copper   limestone   silver   flint   zinc   slate

Write **rock** and **metal** as headings in your book.
Put the words under the right heading.
Use a dictionary to help you.

Chinese tales

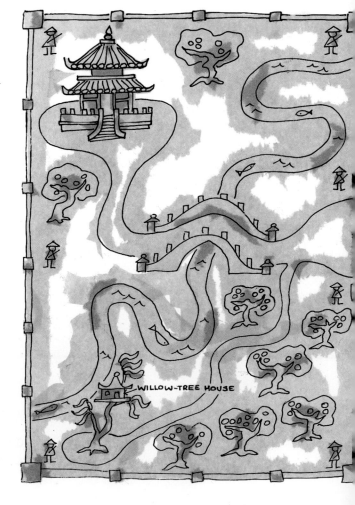

A Chinese story

Once upon a time, long ago, there lived an old Chinaman who had a beautiful house and a beautiful garden. He was very, very rich but he was also very, very mean and never gave anything away.

The old Chinaman had a beautiful daughter called Koong-see who was in love with a poor young man called Chang. Her father sent Chang away because he would not let her marry anyone who was not as rich as he was. He wanted her to marry Ta-jin, one of his rich neighbours.

He told his servants to build a high wooden fence around his land so that no one could get in. He locked Koong-see in a willow-tree house and said that she would stay there until her marriage to Ta-jin. Now Ta-jin was very rich but he was also very fat and very old.

Koong-see was very sad. She sat in the willow-tree house hoping that Chang would come back for her. One day she saw a tiny boat coming towards her on the stream. Inside the boat was a message from Chang telling her to be brave and to get ready to escape with him.

Next day Ta-jin arrived. The old Chinaman had invited a lot of people to welcome Ta-jin so no one saw Chang slip in through the gates and hide in the trees until it was dark . . .

WILLOW-TREE HOUSE

Look at the plan of the old Chinaman's land.
All around the land is a fence that is too high to climb.
There are lots of guards around the fence and at the gate.
How will Chang rescue Koong-see?

● Will they get away? If they do, where will they go?
● Will they get caught? If they do, what will happen to them?

Finish the story.

CHARACTERS IN STORIES

Stories have people or animals in them.
These are called **characters** in the story.
The characters in 'A Chinese story' are the Chinaman,
Koong-see, Chang and Ta-jin.
As we read the story we find out what these characters look
like and what sort of people they are.
Copy the chart and fill it in. The first one is done for you.

Character	What they look like	What sort of person
Chinaman	old	rich, mean
Koong-see		
Chang		
Ta-jin		

PLANNING A STORY – WHO IS IN IT?

Before you write a story you need to plan **who** is in it.
What do your characters look like?
What sort of people are they?

Think about a story you could write called 'The Holiday'.
Your story might include real or imaginary characters.
Think of three characters you could have in your story.

● Write their names.
● Write about what they look like.
● Write about what sort of characters they are.

Record it as a chart like you did for the characters in
'A Chinese story'.

37

A tragic story

There lived a sage in days of yore,
And he a handsome pigtail wore:
But wondered much and sorrowed more
   Because it hung behind him.

He mused upon this curious case,
And swore he'd change the pigtail's place,
And have it hanging at his face,
   Not dangling there behind him.

Says he, "The mystery I've found –
I'll turn me round" – he turned him round;
   But still it hung behind him.

Then round, and round, and out and in,
All day the puzzled sage did spin;
In vain – it mattered not a pin –
   The pigtail hung behind him.

And right and left, and round about,
And up and down, and in and out,
He turned; but still the pigtail stout
   Hung steadily behind him.

And though his efforts never slack,
And though he twist, and twirl, and tack,
Alas! still faithful to his back,
   The pigtail hangs behind him.
               W. M. Thackeray

Glossary

a *sage* is a wise man
yore means long ago
muse means to think deeply

COMPREHENSION   Read the poem and answer the questions.

1 What did the sage want to do?

2 How did he think he had solved the mystery?

3 Do you think the sage was wise or silly?

4 How could he have got the pigtail to hang in front?

A NUMBER OF CHINESE THINGS

Long ago in China, men wore their hair in pigtails.
Not many do today.
Some things in China have not changed.
Look at the pictures.

rickshaws

Great Wall of China

paddy fields

chopsticks

What do you know about the things in the pictures?
What can you find out about them?
Write a sentence for each one.

WORKING WITH WORDS

Chinese people come from **China**.
Can you match the right sort of people with the right country?

Wales	Indian
France	Greek
Greece	Scottish
India	Irish
Ireland	French
Scotland	Welsh

Fairy-tale castles

The fisherman and his wife

One day a poor fisherman catches a magic fish. The fisherman's wife wants to live in a stone castle and the magic fish makes the wish come true.

The fisherman and his wife went to the castle that the magic fish had given them to live in. It was a huge, stone castle with ivy growing up the walls. There were a lot of servants and a lot of rooms. All the rooms had beautiful furniture. The chairs and tables were made of gold. Behind the castle there was a lovely garden and a huge wood. They saw sheep, goats, hares and deer. In the castle courtyard there were stables and cow houses. It really was a wonderful place.

Glossary
courtyard means a space with buildings around it

COMPREHENSION   Read the passage and answer the questions.

1 What did the castle look like from the outside?

2 What was in the rooms of the castle?

3 What did the furniture look like?

4 What was behind the castle?

Not all castles in fairy tales are quite so wonderful as the fisherman's castle.

The Snow Queen

Gerda is looking for her brother Kay. He has been taken away by the wicked Snow Queen. While Gerda is looking for him she is captured by some robbers and taken to their castle.

Suddenly the carriage stopped. They had reached the courtyard of the robbers' castle. Its walls were cracked from top to bottom. Crows and ravens were flying out of the gaps and holes. Huge hounds, each one looking as if he could swallow a man, leapt high into the air, but not a single bark came from them, for that was forbidden. In the great old hall, cobwebbed and black with soot, a large fire burnt on the stone floor. The smoke drifted about under the roof, trying to find its own way out. A vast cauldron of soup was bubbling away. Hares and rabbits were roasting on turning-spits.

Adapted from *The Snow Queen* by Hans Christian Andersen, translated by Naomi Lewis

Glossary
forbidden means not allowed
vast means very big

COMPREHENSION   Read the passage and answer the questions.

1   What words and phrases describe the castle?

2   Write a list of the things inside the castle.

PLANNING A STORY – WHERE DOES IT HAPPEN?

Before you begin to write a story you need to plan **where** the story happens.
This is called the **setting**.

The **setting** for part of 'The fisherman and his wife' is a stone castle with beautiful furniture, a lovely garden and a huge wood.
The **setting** for part of 'The Snow Queen' is an old castle with a cobwebbed, black hall which is very smoky.

Think about a story you could write called 'Trapped'.
Think about the **setting** for your story.

- Where are you trapped?
  It could be in a castle under attack, a tunnel,
  a lift or a crashed car.
  You may have a better idea!
- What sort of things are there around you?

Write a list of words and phrases that describe where you are.

USING BOOK COVERS

Here are the front covers of some story books.
Write one or two sentences to describe the setting for each story.

WORKING WITH WORDS

In the fisherman's castle there is **beautiful** furniture and a **lovely** garden.

In the robbers' castle there is a **large** fire and a **vast** cauldron.

Beautiful and **lovely** mean nice to look at.

Large and **vast** mean very big.

Look at the words in the box.

huge	cute	massive	pretty
handsome	attractive	enormous	gigantic

1 Make a list of the words that mean nice to look at.

2 Make a list of the words that mean very big.

3 Use two 'nice to look at' words in sentences of your own.

4 Use two 'very big' words in sentences of your own.

43

Tudor kings and queens

A family tree

This family tree shows the Tudor kings and queens.

1st line		Henry VII **m** Elizabeth of York			
		r 1485 - 1509 d 1503			

2nd line

Arthur	Henry VIII	Margaret Tudor	Mary Tudor
d 1502	**r** 1509 - 47	**d** 1541	**d** 1533

m

3rd line

1 Catherine of Aragon	2 Anne Boleyn	3 Jane Seymour	4 Anne of Cleves	5 Catherine Howard	6 Catherine Parr
d 1536	**d** 1536	**d** 1537	**d** 1557	**d** 1542	**d** 1548

4th line

Mary I	Elizabeth I	Edward VI
r 1553-58	**r** 1558 -1603	**r** 1547 - 53

m means married
r means reigned or ruled
d means died

COMPREHENSION   Start at the top with Henry VII and answer the questions.

1st line

1 Who did Henry VII marry?

2 When did Henry VII's wife die?

2nd line

3 What was the name of Henry VII's first son?

4 What was the name of his second son?

5 How many daughters did he have?

3rd line

6 How many times did Henry VIII get married?

7 Who was his first wife?

4th line

8 Who was the mother of Mary I?

9 Who was the mother of Elizabeth I?

10 Who was the mother of Edward VI?

BOOK TITLES

We can find out about the people in the family tree by looking at books about the Tudors.

These books will also tell us about the ordinary people and how they lived, as well as about the kings and queens.

Look at these books:

These books are called **factual** or **non-fiction** books.

They tell us about things that really happened.

The title on the front of a book helps us to know what the book is about.

The name on the front of the book is the **author's name**.

The **author** is the person who wrote the book.

USING THE COVERS

Look at the books again.

1 Which book will tell you about homes in Tudor times?

2 Which book will tell you about ships in Tudor times?

3 Which books will tell you about Elizabeth I?

4 Which book will tell you about Anne of Cleves?
   (Look at the family tree again!)

DESIGNING A BOOK COVER

1 Choose one of the people from the Tudor family tree.
Draw a cover for a book about that person.
Write a **title** on your book so people know what it is about.
Write the **author's name** so people know who wrote it.

2 Where else might you find the **author** and **title** on the outside of a book?

THE CONTENTS

Near the beginning of a book you may find the **contents** page.
This page tells you what you will find in the book and on which pages.
Each **chapter** of a book tells you about different things.
This is the contents page from a book called *The Tudors*.

Contents

		Page
Chapter 1	How People Lived	5
Chapter 2	The Kings and Queens	20
Chapter 3	Sailors and Sailing	32
Chapter 4	Wars	45
Chapter 5	Religion	56

Look at the **contents** page and answer the questions.

1 In which chapter could you read about Henry VIII?

2 On what page does chapter 3 begin?

3 How many pages are there in chapter 4?

4 How many pages are there in chapter 1?

5 In which chapter would you be most interested? Why?

THE INDEX

At the back of a factual book you may find an index.
This is a list of the things in the book.
It is written in alphabetical order with the page numbers to look at.

This is part of the index from a book called *Tudor Times*.

	Page
Anne Boleyn	28
Anne of Cleves	30
armour	2
beggars	8
clothes	10
Elizabeth I	32
food	13
Henry VII	1
Henry VIII	15
houses	12

USING THE INDEX   Look at the index and answer the questions.

1 Which page will tell you about clothes?

2 Which page will tell you about Anne of Cleves?

3 What will you find out about by reading page 13?

4 What will you find out about by reading page 2?

5 What will you find out about by reading page 8?

WORKING WITH WORDS

In the time of the Tudors and Stuarts, people were very interested
in learning about such things as the Earth and the human body.
They found out lots of new things and needed new words to
describe them. They made their new words out of words from the
old languages of Latin and Greek.

Look:

atmosphere	Greek	atmos = air	sphaira = sphere
skeleton	Greek	skeleton = dried body	
gravity	Latin	gravis = heavy	
encyclopedia	Greek	enkyklios = circular	paideia = instructions

Look up the red words in your dictionary and write out the meanings.

The diary of Samuel Pepys

Samuel Pepys lived in London and kept a diary at a time when Charles II was king. During Charles' reign there were some disasters which Samuel Pepys recorded in his diary.

In the summer of 1665, London was hit by disease that spread very quickly. This disease was known as the Plague. Thousands of people died. Samuel Pepys wrote about it in his diary.

June 7th This day I did in Drury Lane see two or three houses marked with a red cross upon the doors and 'Lord have mercy upon us' writ there, which was a sad sight to me.

June 21st I find all the town almost going out of town, the coaches and waggons being all full of people going into the country.

The following year, 1666, another disaster hit London which came to be known as the Great Fire. Samuel Pepys wrote about it in his diary.

September 2nd Jane called us up about 3 in the morning, to tell us of a great fire they saw in the City. So I rose and slipped on my nightgown and went to her window . . . By and by, Jane comes and tells us that she hears that above 300 houses have been burned down by the fire and that it is now burning down all Fish Street.

. . . so down, with heart full of trouble, to the Lieutenant of the Tower, who tells me that it began this morning in the King's baker's house in Pudding Lane . . . So I down to the waterside, everybody endeavouring to remove their goods and flinging them into the river . . .

. . . poor people staying in their houses as long as till the very fire touched them, and then running into boats or clambering from one pair of stairs by the waterside, to another . . .

Glossary

reign means to rule as king or queen

a *lieutenant* is an officer in the army

endeavouring means trying

clambering means climbing using hands and feet

COMPREHENSION

Read the passage and answer the questions.

1 Who was king when Samuel Pepys wrote his diary?

2 In what year did the Plague happen?

3 In what year was the Great Fire?

4 What do you think a red cross on a door meant?

5 How did Samuel Pepys feel when he saw the red crosses?

6 Where did the fire start?

7 How did Samuel Pepys feel when he heard about the fire?

8 Why were people throwing their things into the river?

WRITING A DIARY

People keep diaries to record things that happen each day, or to remind them of things that are going to happen.

The diary of Samuel Pepys is full of important events. Most people write about very ordinary things and how they feel about what has happened.

Look at Kim's diary.

Sunday	Rained all day. Bored!
Monday	Back to school after the summer holidays.
Tuesday	4.30 – dentist
Wednesday	Spelling test!
Thursday	Had to go shopping after school with Mum. I hate shopping.
Friday	Went to Ali's for tea. Had a great time.
Saturday	Gran and Grandad came for the day.

COMPREHENSION

Answer these questions about Kim's diary.

1 What did Kim do on Tuesday?

2 What did Kim do on Thursday?

3 How did she feel about it?

4 On which day did Kim have a great time? Why?

5 On which day was Kim bored? Why?

SAM'S DIARY

These pictures show you what Sam did in one week of his summer holidays.

Sunday	Monday	Tuesday

Wednesday   Thursday

Friday   Saturday

Pretend you are Sam. Write his diary for the week.
Begin like this:

Sunday   I helped Mum in the garden today.

WORKING WITH WORDS

The diary of Samuel Pepys is famous because it tells us lots
of things about life in the 17th century.
He is a famous **diarist**.

Can you write these words?
They all end in **ist** and the first letter is given to you.

1 Someone who plays the piano?   p - - - - - -

2 Someone who draws cartoons?   c - - - - - - - -

3 Someone who draws or paints pictures or makes
   other beautiful things such as pottery or statues?   a - - - - -

4 Someone who writes for a newspaper or magazine?   j - - - - - - - -

Up, up and away

People have always been interested in how birds fly and have always wanted to fly themselves. Some of the first attempts to get off the ground were very silly.

The history of flight

From **1783** when the Montgolfier brothers' hot air balloon rose off the ground, mankind has got better and better at finding ways to take to the air.

1797 André Garnerin made the first parachute jump.

1852 Henri Giffard launched the first airship.

1903 The first powered flight. The Wright brothers made four flights in one day. The first lasted 12 seconds and the last 59 seconds.

1907 First helicopter leaves the ground.

1909 Louis Blériot flew across the English Channel.

1919 John Alcock and Arthur Brown flew across the Atlantic in 16 hours and 27 minutes.

1927 Charles Lindbergh made the first solo flight across the Atlantic. His plane was called *Spirit of St Louis*.

1930 Amy Johnson flew solo from England to Australia.

1932 Amelia Earhart was the first woman to fly solo across the Atlantic.

1939 Heinkel He 178 is the first jet to fly.

1969 Concorde made its first flight.

1970 The first jumbo jet flew.

Glossary
solo means alone

COMPREHENSION

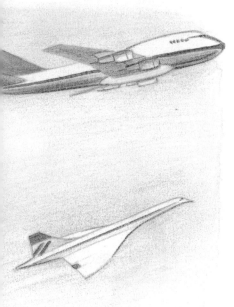

Which of these sentences are right and which are wrong?
Correct the sentences that are wrong.

1　The first successful flight was made by a man with wings.

2　The Montgolfier brothers made the first aeroplane flight.

3　The first parachute jump was made in 1797.

4　The Wright brothers went up in their aeroplane five times in one day.

5　The first helicopter flew in 1907.

6　Alcock and Brown crossed the Atlantic in less than 24 hours.

7　Lindbergh's aeroplane was called *Spirit of St Louis*.

8　Amy Johnson flew solo across the Atlantic.

9　The first jet engine flight was in 1939.

10　Concorde was the first jumbo jet.

A FLYING DIARY!

1　Read about the Wright brothers again.
You might be able to find out more information about them.

2　Now imagine you are one of the Wright brothers.
Write your diary for the day you made the four flights.

Think about how you felt:
● were you excited?
● were you frightened?
Think about what you saw:
● were people watching you?
● what did the Earth look like from up there?
● what did the sky look like?

A SPACE POEM

As well as flying around the world in aeroplanes, people
have now flown right away from the Earth and landed
on the Moon.
Here is one person who would like to travel in space.

Daydreams

I want to be an astronaut,
Play tag among the stars,
Eat cornflakes on the cold, cold Moon,
Bacon and eggs on Mars.

I'd always wear a spacesuit,
Glass helmet on my head,
Oxygen pack upon my back.
Without them I'd be dead.

I'd sail my silver spacecraft
Across the Milky Way;
Then head direct for Venus
Along a gamma ray.

I'd pick up heaps of stardust
On the old Apollo trails,
Stray splinters from a meteor,
Moondust and comets' tails . . .

But these are only daydreams.
My fastest speed to date,
Is home from school in half an hour
On my brother's roller skates.

Charles Connell

The poet talks about things to do with space travel.
Look at the chart.
It shows you a list of words that are in the poem.
Some of them are explained. Use a dictionary and
information books to find out about the other words.

Milky Way	The mass of stars clustered together like a white cloud in the sky.
Venus	The brightest planet we can see from Earth.
Apollo	17 American spacecraft were called Apollo. Apollo 11 landed the first man on the Moon.
comet	Starlike body in the sky with a long tail of light.
astronaut	?
Moon	?
oxygen	?
meteor	?

WORKING WITH WORDS

The photographs show two ways
of travelling through the air.

The hot air balloon travels **slowly**.

The space rocket travels **quickly**.

1 Make a list of **slow** words to describe how the hot air balloon moves.

2 Make a list of **quick** words to describe how the rocket moves.

Why are they famous?

What is an encyclopedia?

An encyclopedia is a reference book which gives us information about many different things.
Most encyclopedias are set out in alphabetical order like a dictionary.

Darling, Grace Born 1815, died 1842. British heroine, daughter of a lighthouse keeper.
In 1838 she helped her father rescue 9 people from a ship that had hit the rocks in a storm.

Dickens, Charles Born 1812, died 1870. British story writer whose famous books include *Oliver Twist*, *A Christmas Carol* and *David Copperfield*.

Disney, Walt Born 1901, died 1966. American film maker. His most famous cartoon character is Mickey Mouse who was created in 1928. Disney's films include *Snow White and the Seven Dwarfs*, *Pinocchio* and *Mary Poppins*.

This information tells us about some famous people.
It tells us:
when they were born
when they died
where they were born
why they are famous

COMPREHENSION

1 When was Grace Darling born?

2 Why is she famous?

3 What is the name of the famous story writer?

4 Where was he born?

5 When did Walt Disney die?

6 Write the names of two of his famous films.

USING AN ENCYCLOPEDIA

When we use an encyclopedia to find out something we do not need to copy every word.
We can make **notes** of the important facts.
Notes do not have to be in sentences.
Look:

Notes on Walt Disney
Born – 1901
Died – 1966
Important things he did – made films such as *Snow White and the Seven Dwarfs*.

1 Make some notes on Grace Darling.

2 Use an encyclopedia to make some notes on **one** of these famous people:

Alfred the Great
(fought against
the Vikings)

The Wright brothers
(made the first
powered flight)

Samuel Pepys
(kept a diary which tells us
about the Plague and the
Great Fire of London)

MORE FAMOUS PEOPLE

People are famous for lots of different things.
Look at this list:

Van Gogh

Queen Elizabeth II

Roald Dahl

Mary Seacole

Shakespeare

Margaret Thatcher

Daley Thompson

Mother Teresa

Enid Blyton

Nelson Mandela

Copy the list into your book and next to each name
write what they are or were famous for.
Where will you find the information you need if you
do not know?

I WANT TO BE FAMOUS

Imagine you are a famous person.
Write about what you are famous for.

- Did you invent something?
- Were you the first person to do something?
- Are you better than anyone else at doing something?
- Do you like being famous?
- What is bad about being well known?

WORKING WITH WORDS

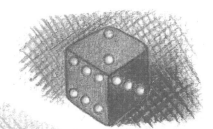

1 Look at the word **encyclopedia**.
  How many words can you make using
  the letters in encyclopedia?
  The pictures will help you with some of the words.
  Here are two to start you off:

  encyclopedia
  cycle
  pen

2 **Fame** is a noun ('naming' word).
  Famous is an adjective ('describing' word).
  By adding **ous** we can make some nouns into adjectives.

  Change these nouns into adjectives by using **ous**.

  danger
  mountain
  courage
  fury
  glory

Use your
dictionary to
check your
spelling.

Did they really live?

Some people are very famous but we can't be certain that they ever really lived. Lots of stories are told about them. These stories are called **legends**.

Robin Hood

There are many legends about Robin Hood. Robin was the son of a nobleman who lived in Locksley in Yorkshire when King Richard I ruled England. The king had to go away to fight a war leaving his evil brother, Prince John, in charge. Prince John took the land and houses of the king's friends and tried to make himself king. He killed Robin's father, but Robin escaped and lived as an outlaw in Sherwood Forest.

Other men who were afraid for their lives joined Robin in the forest to hide from the evil Prince. They are said to have worn green clothes in the forest and to have been very good with bows and arrows.

The stories say that Robin Hood and his men took money from Prince John's friend, the Sheriff of Nottingham. They did not keep the money but gave it back to the poor people who had been made to give it to the Sheriff.

Glossary

outlaw means someone outside the protection of the law

a *sheriff* is an important officer of the law

COMPREHENSION

Read the passage and answer the questions.

1 Why did King Richard leave England?

2 Who was in charge while the king was away?

3 Where did Robin hide?

4 Why did other men hide with him?

5 Why do you think that Robin Hood and his men wore green in the forest?

6 What do you think Robin Hood is best remembered for?

A PICTURE STORY

One day in Summer, Robin Hood and his men were sitting round a camp fire in Sherwood Forest.

Friar Tuck came to tell them that the Sheriff of Nottingham and his men were coming through the forest with lots of money.

Robin and his men got ready to take the money from the Sheriff.

We know **when** the story takes place – one day in Summer.
The **setting** of the story is in a forest.
The **characters** are Robin Hood, his men, Friar Tuck, the Sheriff of Nottingham and his soldiers.

The **plot** so far . . . Friar Tuck comes to tell Robin Hood and his men that the Sheriff of Nottingham and some soldiers are travelling through the forest with lots of money. Robin Hood is going to take the money away from the Sheriff to give it back to the poor people.
How will he do this?

Imagine you are Robin Hood or one of his men.
Finish the story of how you took the money from the Sheriff.
Remember you are in a forest and you have to take the money from a lot of soldiers.

William Tell

Another famous man in legend is William Tell. He lived long ago in a part of Switzerland that was ruled by an evil man called Gessler. William and his friends would not do what Gessler wanted so the evil man punished him.

Gessler tied up William's son and put an apple on his head. William Tell was a good shot with a crossbow which fired bolts. Gessler said he had to shoot the apple off his son's head.

William took two bolts, put one in his belt and one in the crossbow. He shot at the apple and split in in two.

Gessler was angry. He asked William why he had taken two bolts out. William said that if he had killed his son with the first one, he would have killed Gessler with the second. William Tell was arrested and put onto a ship that would take him to prison. He jumped overboard, swam to the shore and escaped.

Glossary

arrested means taken prisoner

COMPREHENSION   Read the passage and answer the questions.

1 What do you think Gessler was thinking as William got ready to shoot at the apple?

2 What do you think William Tell was thinking as he got ready to shoot at the apple?

WHAT WOULD YOU FEEL LIKE?

Imagine you are William Tell's son.
Write about how you feel when:
- you are tied up
- the apple is put on your head
- your father gets ready to shoot at the apple
- the apple is split in two

WORKING WITH WORDS

Look:
famous = well known and honoured
infamous = well known for wicked, shameful things

Lots of words have **in** at the beginning to make their opposites.
Look up these words in your dictionary.
Write their meaning and their opposites:

independent
incorrect
incapable
invisible